BLEEDING GULL

Look, Feel, Fly

RAED ANIS AL-JISHI

PARTRIDGE

A Penguin Random House Company

To order additional copies of this book, contact
Toll Free 800 101 2657 (Singapore)
Toll Free 1 800 81 7340 (Malaysia)
orders.singapore@partridgepublishing.com

www.partridgepublishing.com/singapore

Contents

To My Asmaa

Beginning of the Clay

From the staleness of clay,
I have masks
That could seduce their jailed clouds
In the arrogant ice
Growing on the chosen dust.

The newborn wind's trembling
On a pearl that is covered
With its self-esteem
Between two seas
And one spirit.

Hanging Out

The flower
Refused to wither.
The thorns
Didn't make a melody.
Me, my confusions, and my bread
Exchange our parts in time.
A broken man
Hangs with broken things.

Harmony

The papers of ashes vanished.
The picture became a woman.
Her window smiles.
I feel the harmony with her balcony,
And a crow of death
Caws harmoniously
With us.

Wailer

Oh, wailer,
You are still as you were
With cloudy eyes,
Opening your window's chest
Like a drunkard
Calling one thousand lamps.

And your dreams
Are just tides
Without rising.

Wax Effect

Everyone you called
Was astonished
By your charming lights.

But they forgot
The effect of the wax
On your body.

Leave the no-man's-land.
Take your tombs,
Flutes, and cups with you.
The melodies
Will not live forever.
The trance of emptying your mind
Will not live forever.
Nothing lived.
Nothing will.

Burgundy

Let it out.
Make me elaborate my journey
Between your eyes,
Finding the truth,
Winning the impossible hope.

Where is that burgundy tremor
To delete all the seasons
And live ourselves
As a morning
When the evening
Is coming ahead?

Infant Martyr

Since the night of shoots,
The night of travail,
The call to prayer calms me.
Some people chant,
"Hale Loya."
It was the last supper
And a birth
Of a certain death.

My silicone
Was oxidized with love.
I was born from a companion
Of Al-Jalil dust
And Euphrates water,
And I became
The infant martyr.

Grieve

Are you suffering from
The anxiety of poetry
And the reading pain?

Take my letters.
Share the bread of ink,
Sea, and the salt of the sailors' chants
With me.
Some grief can't end
Till it hurts you more
Than you bear to speak.

Pendulum

I am a pendulum.
The flames burn my body
In the midday.
Then the ice revives me
In the night
To be suitable
For the morning death.

Sleepless in Style

Whenever the desire
Defines me as sleepless
And my letters betray
My silence oath,
I wear the angle
Of the lonely night,
And my hand wears a cup of tea.
Nothing can hide us both
Or hide our climax
But the wing of the darkness.

Riding

I didn't use to ride a cigar
After making love,
But now
I am smoking
A body of tobacco
And a soul of wine.

Who burns who?
Was it me?
Was it the cigar?
Or was it just the smoke of my life
When it got lost
In the era of congestion?

Motivation of Death

We are going to wear
death
When we decorate our dreams
In the salience of the universe
As tales of love
That can rock the emptiness.

Love
Looks like us,
But we went far, far away,
And it is still
Following our traces
In the air.

Praying

If the core of rising
Is the core of kneeling,

Where will I direct
And surrender
My eyes?

Innocent Eyes

Playing a lute
In the middle of the lure,
Wearing the layout of sprays,
The innocent-eyed girl
Weaves her feather
As a wing of peregrination
In the meaning of utterance.
She shakes out the cheek
Of relegation
When her foliar fortress
Refuses to bare the feelings
From her friction
That has been crossed
On the slabs
Of the veil.

Smiling

And I smile
Not because of joy
I usually sip in morning
But to deceive
The wrinkle lines
Cheating on my memory.

Transfiguration

When the distance with stillness
Becomes a ticket for the passengers
And there is no other trip,
The transfiguration's port
Gets caught by
Desertification.
The sound waves
Seduce dreams
And sow the holiday bread
And the flavor of new cotton
While awaiting the holy Eid
On the banks of silence
on the absenteeism's side.

Upside-Down Creature

As wide as patience could be,
I played an anchor's melody
Hanged by its placenta,
Warping my fetus's wishes.

The upside-down creature
In my body
Extends its fingers toward
The reflection of light,
Scratching the mirrors
Of my abdomen.
The refraction of silence
Forsakes it
In the ringing's womb.

Identical

The line of the brunette coffee
Still draws a fist of our heart,
Putting its love into
The windows of latency,
Bringing back the ascendancy of
The poem's body
To the hallucination.
The velvety headache
Flamed him.

And the crawling of
Passion's memory
Becomes nails
In
The metaphor of buzzing.

Qateefy Nature

What is the benefit of
Letting alphabets
Fall as blueberry leaves
Under my legs?
I have a Qateefy nature
Unlike the flower's qualities,
And beside the robbery, looting
My bleeding and dryness,
I am standing still.

Tunisia

A flower
Carried carefully by the wind,
The verses of the petals are
Hymns of morning.
The time dreams about
The flowing of dew's intonation
As a perfume above her cheeks
On the tuning of green.
That is the dream,
And the foam of its flavor
Is a spring of fragrance
And freedom.

Learning

I am ripping
The Ten Commandments' lamp.
The demon is a fastened sea
With a sealed window,
And when I get dazed,
I forget the amusement
Of slipping on the stones of thoughts
And the flavor of sterilizing
My wrist.

Turbans

Our cotton
Didn't take the side
Of the sun
Anymore.
The twisted sweat
Is not injected inside us
As a shiver of a poem's smoke.
We are shaved-off sugar
And dreams
In the chaos era of turbans.

The Message

Our poetry invents
The message of cawing,
But we don't care
If the psalm's olive
Didn't choose the prophet crow
And got deceived by
The harmony
Of a dancing pigeon.

Memory's Lisp

I stand nearby me
Watching that guy
Come from the land far away.
We have the same lisp
In our tongue and memory.
He went through me,
And I didn't notice
He stole my poems
And placed a knife
On the flank of my lips.

An Affair

The frozen water
In my eyes,
Which was scratched by
A cat of time,
Is changing my spring
That I desire,
My vinegary dreams,
And the songs that love me
Into
A one-night affair.

Aging Love

The language of love
Is spontaneity like me,
Like a painting of a kid.
I used to draw my house
On the left side of the paper.
My house was so small,
Neither doors nor windows
On the sand of aging.

Beirut Nights

I am gambling
In Beirut nights.
I need two numbers.
Melt together.
Never asked any die
About its color,
Where it was made,
And its birthday
In gambling.

Some gambling is
The red line of revolutions,
A dot of enlightenment,
And a calendar of life.

DJ

I don't need
A parasite guitar
To adjust
The hymns of the sky
With a stranger
Melody.

Demonstrations

Astonished,
The gunpowder
Talks behind your back.
From which pride
Did God
Puddle your hands?

Whenever you send them
Up to death,
Death kneels like heaven
And worships you.

Prisoner

Surrounded by the walls of memory
With no lover
And nothing to remember,
I am mocking
My triangle cuffs
And the illusions
Of the circle hands.
There is an iron cage
Of emotions
And a jail of
Ironic melodies.

Jailed but Free

I roll up.
I smoke the minute's pulses.
I inject the heroin of
love into my veins
No one can shut me up.
My flying poems
Hide themselves
In the packets of hearts,
Seeding their papaver
In their cells
To grow just like my words
drunk
And crazy.

Homeland Songs

It is okay, my home,
If I hug you.
When you enter my body,
Every street and corner
Becomes a dream of an artery.
You can pick all the grapes
In my vine heart
Even if you shoot me
With your dancing bullets.

My Right

It is my right
To love as she wants,
To get ripped by desires
When her necklace scattered as
Tears of pearls.
It is a riot,
And it is my right
To love and die
As she wants.

Gypsy Souls

My soul
Is my gypsy poems.
My home
Is my foreignness
On the novel's wagon.
I don't sell
The razor tickets,
The dance of a free bra,
Or my cigar of passionate dreams
When I smoke the verses
And spread their sunflower hulls
To lead
The wandering souls.

My Way

They said
I was born from foam,
Foam that was yeast
From the silver
Of a fish,
A fish that escaped from
A gull's hand,
A gull that couldn't bear
The chants of the gulf,
And that is why
I couldn't swim with or against
The pawing of the waves
Nor fly away from the language
Of the uproar,
But that is my way,
And my way is mine.

Religion Is Love

Distances are empty
Between us.
Prayers are love,
And when I get drunk
By desire,
I forget from which amulet
I wrote myself
By its bloody saffron
And by which one
I erase me.

Red is another language,
And I can speak
No more.

Anti-Beta Aquarii

I don't care
About being related to one
Beta Aquarii
To become an ambassador
For a strange sand
Or to perfect my ecstasy
When my need for singing
Betrays me.

Visions

And I see
Pieces of charity
Falling down from
Gull-crucified bread
To feed the inspectors' rats,

And I see
Rats bullying
The refraction of rays,
Thinking that
They were
The source of lighting
In the clay.

Sinners

Chaos lives inside us.
We are practicing our sins
To regain the feeling
Of being human.
Our blood vessels
Cannot weave sails
For the traveling days,
Nor feathers for
The falling angels.

Crucified Languages

In the theater of time,
Crucified on my language,
Watching the birds
Falling on my song,
Stealing the pieces of bread
From my melody,
What does the significance
Prepare for me?
Its tones' nails
Bleed my rhyming soul
While its hopes shatter my hands,
And my questions couldn't
Hammer any dream.

A Habit

My habit is being free,
And it could torture me
And could stitch the silence wax
In my lips.
But I am sending myself
By hiding my letters
In the scent of my
guillotine's flowers.

Stolen Wadis

Those who emigrate to my heart
Wear hard rock claws,
Digging their eyes
Between the tents
And the bleeding flowers,
Exploring the wadi
Of the stolen wishes.

Blindness

Their identikits are a mystery.
I couldn't recognize them
By the reflection
Of the winds
Nor the censors
On my blind stick.
They went through me
With sympathy.
"Your son looks like you,"
One of them said,
Leaving me
On the pavement of silence.
What does he look like?
Did he like it?
What do I look like?
What is the meaning of identikits?
Why can't I
Have a simple answer
For a simple question?
What is the difference between
White and black?

Exposed

The specks of dust climbs
The wooden chair
In the body of winter
On the turning point
Of the high road,

Growing up
Like a wailing fig,
Wearing its stripping,
And dancing
With the handsome light
Of the moon.

Sometimes
Being nude
Is being proud
Of standing alone.

That Same Life

I was in that same place.
I practiced that same life.

So why every time
Did the wind
Kill my steps,
Strew my tulip origins,
Seeding the time?

Why did the time collect me
As tears of bleeding wax,
Reviving my Apollo skin,
Reviving me?

I was in that same place.
I practiced that same life.

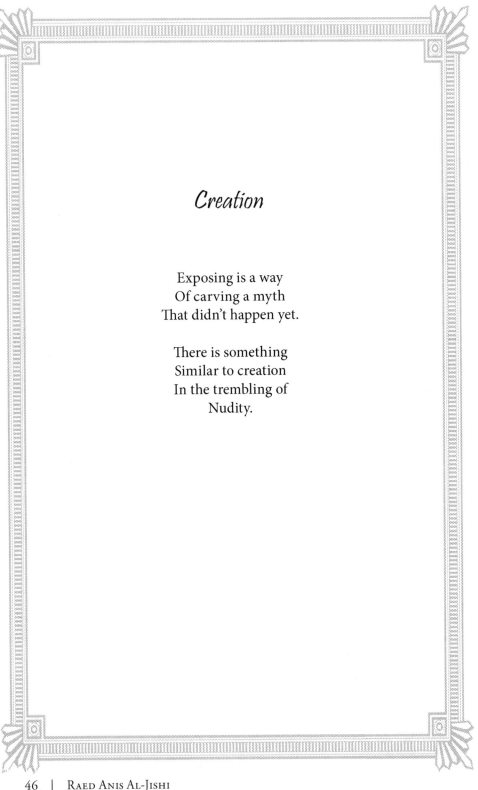

Creation

Exposing is a way
Of carving a myth
That didn't happen yet.

There is something
Similar to creation
In the trembling of
Nudity.

Hope

Empty
From all the lamps' hopes
And what the god of stories
Pours in our water soul,

Looking for the blueness
In the sky
To treat the cracks of heaven
With my oily tones.

The Fifth Gate

I have four open gates
In my heart,
Four different pulses
Of neighing.
The first horseman
Is from
The frozen emotions
With an empty bow.
No arrow can break its ice.
The second is from
The dawn of desire.
No one
Can feed its hunger for love.
The third is from
The black hole of silence,
Counting rapidly
The falling hours.
The fourth is from
The winds of hope
That couldn't blow
My hallow
Smile.

Gulls' Chants

I drink
The low-fat morning death.
I start it with eating dates.
How many times did
The dates immigrate us?

How many times did they strip
The conscience of silence
By the locusts of sand?

Locusts that can't understand
The chants of the gulls
Or the whispers
Of the sea waves

Dilmun

And I see
Peasants
Singing in the milky road
With a bull
That didn't know
What the plow looks like.

And beggars
Desert sharpeners
Like a flock of chitin strings
Bleeding their wounds
With long red beards,
Hooked noses,
And a mass of noise.

Singing

And I was singing
While the slave cells
Dance around me.
They wet the cotton of seduction
When I moved my head
As a poem,
And my letters
Went so deep through
Their climax souls.

Seeking

Where
Will the silence lead you?
Ishtar closed her wine.
The fence is growing on the port.
You didn't use to get drunk
And couldn't swim that good.
Look at the flammable waves
And your trembling legs.
You are going to live forever.
You are going to die tomorrow.
So what is the benefit
Of being away?

Twinkling

I left my logic and questioning
To play like a kid
With a drop of water,
Drawing whatever
Your deep black sea wants.

Your eyes are the windows
That can contain
All the borders' shades
In that whole universe.

The East Gate

As a darwich,
I am flattered by poems, emotions,
Spitting the coffea
In the longing coffee.

From the east,
The last gate of escaping,
I looked upon us
In the bubbles.
I saw us
In the reflection
Of a young color,
Singing the impossible
In the womb of
The extinction angle.

Wide Open

Wide open,
I don't mind
If the overwhelmed poets
Go through my heart
And eat
From the grapes.

In the presence of poetry,
The drops of blood
Are prayers,
And the drops of prayers
Are blood
Nothing less,
Nothing more.

Love Road

From the light,
They were born
As waves of a dream,
Dry on the faces of the shore
When the city melted,
Desiring poetry.
Nothing could color the faces
But the shades of the raptors.
They love till they forget
When they put their first step
And what is their goal.

Believing

The steps
Are their traces on
The pink clouds,
But they don't lead to them.
The small tombs
Cover the number
Of their shoes.

Inana's Joy

Clouds witnessed
Inana's tears of joy
When she laid back on
The merciful tree
And liked
What the sailors saw
Between her legs:
A grass of wisdom,
An infant rose,
And a chant of life
On Tarout's gulf.

Masks

I cannot recognize myself
If I don't wear me.
Faces are deceiving
Without their masks,
Like that bleeding
White gulf.

Martyrs

By the horses
That look like martyrs,
When they flatter with
The scent of the hill,
Seduced by heavenly apples,
An aroma
Of pride coos.

The Holy Book

In the beginning
Love was a gift from God.
Its law melts as words.
Its eve was the tones
In the letters.
No Adam was there
But
A sheet that contains
The fate of
All lovers.

Fatimah

Something was shattered
On the twilight of her eyes,
The cornelian flow
Raising one thousand questions
without answers.

Her secret prayers
Were hidden
In a tomb of night,
And the dust
Cleans its traces.

Serving a Smile

We have a bashful tradition
In hospitality.
Our Arabian coffee
Does not need sugar
Or cardamom
To be tasty or lovable
Just like the smile
We serve
To all the passersby.

Imam Husayn

Like a stem cell,
The infant universe
Grows inside you
Like a martyr star.
You will die
But your lights
Will live forever.
And like a sumer[1] cup,
You will die thirsty
While the rivers of life
Will always rise
From your hand.

---

[1] An ancient civilization.

Third Eye

There is a holy spot
Between her eyes
Where
Angels burn their feathers
And lose their faith.

Blame me not.

Wrinkles

The wrinkles
Choose their boards,
The size of their brushes,
And their colors
To steal all the stories
Of our life
And bury them
In the maze of holes.
Like death,
They can erase
All the sins
That will never repent.

Writing has the rituals
Of scars.

Newton's Law of Love

On a swirl of time,
Accidentally we met.
Love stimulates
Our steps
To create the gulls' melodies
Dancing on the shore.

A prayer
Confuses the sun,
So she moves around us,
Learning from our heart language
How to fall forever
And ever
In love.

Gray

She hides her puberty.
Her tears
Were about to expose her,
But she appeals
For the silent help,
Standing in front of a mirror,
Asking her colored shadow,
"What could happen
If we exchange our places?
Or if we unite
In the traveling light?"
You are like me.
Everything inside you is
Shallow
Between the eyes
Of
The tribe.

Autism Girls

An autism girl
Searching for the spring
Between the black clouds

Her braids are made
From a shining rose.
Her dreams are made
From a shining rose.
But who could listen
To the scent?

Her smile
Could light the darkness,
But one question bridled her.

Why are they using (her)
When they talk about me?

Am I vanished?!
Am I?
A hush—
Then she melts
Like a flower in the snow.

Stranger Citizens

They vanished
Like our palm trees,
Ancient free windows,
And old dreams.

The city forgot their names
While they were holding its memory
In the soul
As a candle
Between
The prison bars.

Hero

My love poem's horse
Died standing.

And as a freed prisoner,
I came back home
As a hero,
But my soul
Stayed with my friends
in prison.

"Why am I the only one alive?"
Is torturing me.
Love is my sin.
Love is my curse.

The Aroma of Hopes

She stood looking through
The newspaper
Behind the window of ashes

Her eyes
Listened to his steps sound.

What could the skin say
In the language of shoes?

She could see through
His smile's membranes
And expose the scent
Of her broken hopes.

First Step

Your first steps
Are my undefined tears.
They stripped my heart.
My naked pulses stuttered.
Their light was focusing on
The greatest finishing move
In our play.

There must be
A new definition
For love
In my virgin dictionary.

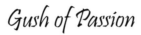

Gush of Passion

I am combing melody's hair,
Buttoning its new shirt
Because,
When the poem
Becomes a woman,
I become the gush of light
And my verses become
A holiday hour's.
But when the poem
Becomes you,
I become the martyr passion.

Buttons

Button by button,
Like a martyr's mantis
Shattered by making mortality
Or a paralyzed hand monk,
His eyes still hugging heaven,
We fall in love.

In spite of the heavy water,
We are wearing the bubble,
Shutting the eyes of life,
Drinking from ourselves
Till the end.

A Cup of Hope

The time
Is one hour of hope's tea
And fifteen dropped minutes
Of honey.

Waiting is rushing
In my veins,
Yellow but not that pale,
Feeding my cells with
A flammable desire.

Mitochondria

My mitochondria
Declare their rebellion,
Tear my soul,
Send it to the deficit exile,
Welcoming the newborn
Phoenix.

I can see myself there
On a flame.
I can see myself here
As nothing.
Yet they chose another human
As a host.

Who stole the revolution?

On the Edge

The thought stood on the edge
Of my tongue
And jumped.
What is the benefit of the sea?
Even if it understands
Why the birds migrate from his body,
If the fog surrounded to
The shore.

A Stranger Gull

The sea has long fingers,
And like history
It covers
The roughness of the sand.

Its waves hide the heat
Like a broken and a gloomy
Cup of tea.

I spit an old desire of
Chewing tobacco
Before drinking,
And as a stranger gull,
I fly
Against its wind.

Imazigh

I am a Tuareg's child.
My blue turban drowns me
In the waves of sadness,
Then throws me up
As a seed of ivory.

Oh, great Tin Hinan,
Your brave knight
Lost his way between
The salt caravans.
Imazighen is free
No more.

A Summer Day

Unlike Shakespearian verses,
I felt the summer day.
The sun burned
My nightly wings,
And the wind threw me away.
My steps on the milky shore,
My feathers in the sky,
Drawing a Picasso painting,
Raising,
"What? Who cares?
And why?"

Cat

Riding your high horse
With an iron fist,
Fearing my wet nose.

Rising

Rising from my soul
As hallow as a bubble,
Shallow as a doll.

Broken but Not Done

What a deceptive sea
What a confused land
On beaches' cells,
Love stands,
Singing alone
A sad song
With a broken heart.
There is nothing right.
There is nothing wrong.

Pregnancy

My body usually erupts,
And it hurts me when it erupts.
But it terrifies me
With its painful time delay,
And my legs don't tremor.
My back doesn't moan,
And I don't dig my smile
With whining.
I get used to
That presage
And what it chooses
And nominates.

Breast Cancer

My kid is playing on my hand,
And he stuns me,
How he chooses my right breast
And sucks my age
Till it swells.
I try to astonish him
With my left,
But he rubs its teat
With his hands
And doesn't drink from it.

My child
Flips a thousand meanings
In my teat.
Why is he afraid of the left?
And what terrifies him?

Sadistic Kiss

Your kiss is sadistic.
Your saliva is holy,
And you have Bermuda's eyes.

My compass gets confused,
And I don't know.
Am I seeing the truth
Or the fantasy?

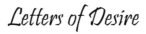

Letters of Desire

My dreams have been generated
From the letters of desire.
I am still growing inside you,
And the fabulous ice
Transformed into hands
Contains me with its climax.
I am in a nebula of light.
I don't see anything
But you
As a warming source.

Ra'ed Anis Al-jishi

thebleedinggull@hotmail.com
raedaljishi@gmail.com
https://twitter.com/aljishiraed
https://www.facebook.com/aljishiraed

Tel – 00966566319889
P.O.Box- 60070
Al-Qateef – 31911
Saudi Arabia